20TH CENTURY
fashion
THE 40^S & 50_S
UTILITY *to* NEW LOOK

Please visit our web site at: www.garethstevens.com
For a free color catalog describing Gareth Stevens Publishing's list of high-quality books
and multimedia programs, call 1-800-542-2595 (USA) or 1-800-461-9120 (Canada).
Gareth Stevens Publishing's Fax: (414) 332-3567.

Library of Congress Cataloging-in-Publication Data

Reynolds, Helen.
    The 40s & 50s: utility to new look / by Helen Reynolds.
      p. cm. — (20th century fashion)
    Includes bibliographical references and index.
    Summary: Traces changes in fashion during the 40s and 50s including military styles, utility clothes,
Dior glamour, and the modernist look.
    ISBN 0-8368-2600-0 (lib. bdg.)
    1. Fashion—History—20th century—Juvenile literature. 2. Nineteen forties. 3. Nineteen fifties.
[1. Fashion—History—20th century. 2. Nineteen forties. 3. Nineteen fifties.] I. Title. II. Series.
GT596.R49   2000
391'.009'044—dc21   99-054430

This North American edition first published in 2000 by
Gareth Stevens Publishing
A World Almanac Education Group Company
330 West Olive Street, Suite 100
Milwaukee, Wisconsin 53212 USA

Original edition © 1999 by David West Children's Books. First published in Great Britain in 1999
by Heinemann Library, Halley Court, Jordan Hill, Oxford OX2 8EJ, a division of Reed Educational
and Professional Publishing Limited. This U.S. edition © 2000 by Gareth Stevens, Inc. Additional
end matter © 2000 by Gareth Stevens, Inc.

Editor: Clare Oliver
Picture Research: Carlotta Cooper/Brooks Krikler Research

Gareth Stevens Series Editor: Dorothy L. Gibbs

Photo Credits:
Abbreviations: (t) top, (m) middle, (b) bottom, (l) left, (r) right

Corbis: pages 16(bl), 20(r), 23(ml), 25(l)
Mary Evans Picture Library: page 27(tr)
Hulton Getty: Cover (m), pages 5(tr), 6(tl, bl), 7(tr), 8(tl, r), 10-11, 11(tr, bm, br), 12(bl), 13(tl, tr),
15(tr), 17(br), 19(tr1, tr2), 20(l), 21(tl), 22(bl), 25(br), 28(tr, br), 28-29, 29(bl)
Kobal Collection: pages 5(tl), 15(b), 21(tr), 24(tl), 26(tr)
Pictorial Press: pages 5(bl), 6(br), 7(bl), 9(tr), 12(tl), 13(br), 21(bl), 22-23, 23(br), 26(bl)
Redferns: Cover (tr, br), pages 3(br), 12-13, 24(bl), 24-25, 25(tr), 26(tl), 27(br, bl)
© *Vogue*/Condé Nast Publications Ltd / Cecil Beaton: pages 5(mr), 10(bl), 16(br), 19(br) /
Blumenfeld: pages 18-19 / Rene Bouche: pages 16-17 / Rene Bouet-Willeumez: page 9(br2) /
Henry Clarke: page 4(mr) / Coffin: page 19(bl) / Carl Erickson: page 18(tl) / Piguet: page 18(bl) /
Rawlings: Cover (bl), pages 3(tr), 9(ml), 15(tl) / Renovations: page 9(br1) / Seeberger: page 16(tl) /
Vernier: page 29(tr) / *Vogue* Magazine: Cover (tl, bm), pages 3(tl), 10(tl), 14(tl, bm), 17(tr), 18(br) /
Caradog Williams: page 23(tr)

With special thanks to the Picture Library and Syndication Department at *Vogue* Magazine/Condé
Nast Publications Ltd.

Printed in Mexico

2 3 4 5 6 7 8 9 05 04 03 02 01

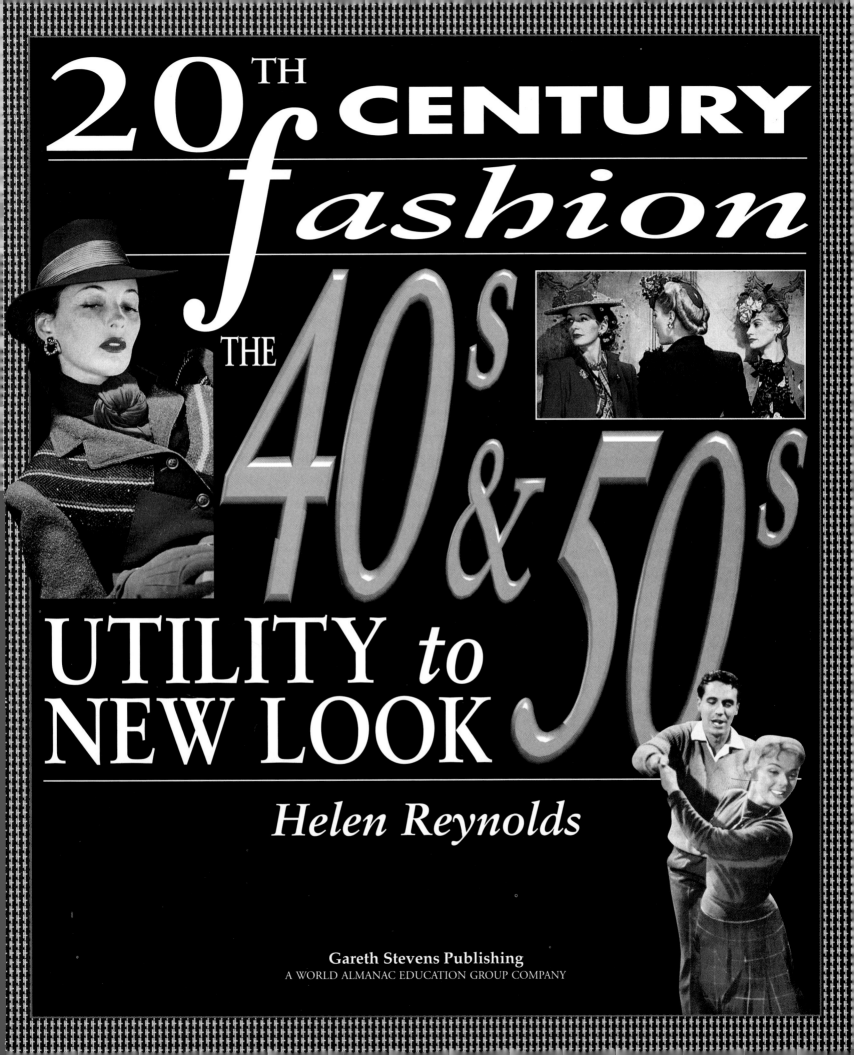

20TH CENTURY

fashion

THE 40s & 50s

UTILITY *to* NEW LOOK

Helen Reynolds

Gareth Stevens Publishing
A WORLD ALMANAC EDUCATION GROUP COMPANY

Contents

By the late 1950s, women in search of comfort moved away from the constrictions of Dior's New Look. This stylish Chanel suit (1958) is made of easy-to-wear jersey.

The United States was the birthplace of youth crazes. At coffee houses and soda fountains, teenagers showed off their newest clothes and danced to the jukebox sounds of the latest pop hits.

The Hard 1940s and the Rocking 1950s

The 1940s and 1950s were years of momentous changes, and most of them stemmed from the unusual circumstances of World War II. As men fought, women performed traditionally male jobs, for which they needed practical clothing.

Betty Grable was the pinup queen. Her legs were insured for a million dollars!

Styles during the war were durable and sensible. Out of necessity, people began to accept that mass-produced clothing could be as fashionable as haute couture. Top fashion magazines, such as *Vogue*, displayed factory-made, ready-to-wear garments alongside couture. Glamour was confined to movie screens and the pinup photos that kept up the morale of servicemen far from home.

Clothes were rationed, so they had to be versatile. This light, woolen dress (1943) could be worn year round.

When the war was over, women reacted against many years of "making do." Christian Dior presented his New Look in February 1947. Before long, this feminine silhouette of full skirts, tight waists, and sloping shoulders had filtered down into mainstream fashion.

From the beginning, women did their part for the war effort. These WAAFs (Women's Auxiliary Air Force) are loading an RAF truck.

After the war, when husbands and wives were reunited, there was a baby boom. By the prosperous fifties, these babies were teenagers, who eagerly developed their own culture and style. From the time rock 'n' roll was born in 1955, music and youth fashion remained closely linked.

The fifties were years of great excitement. An explosion of new technology made anything seem possible. By the end of the decade, the silicon chip had been invented, and the first satellite had been launched successfully into space. A new age was about to begin.

Fashions of War

At the dawn of the 1940s, Europe was already three months into World War II (1939–1945). For the first half of the decade, fashion took a back seat as every available person and material was pulled into the war effort.

Members of the Women's Auxiliary Air Force (WAAF) had to learn new skills. Practicality was more important than femininity.

THE HOME FRONT

At first, only women without family commitments were recruited for war work. They worked on farms and in factories, and they nursed in the hospitals that sprang up to serve the fighting forces. Before long, nurseries and child-care facilities freed more women for essential war work.

JOINING UP

Women were encouraged to help the war effort directly. Whether they joined land, sea, or air forces, and whether they were on the side of the allies or the Axis powers of Germany, Italy, and, later, Japan, military women all wore uniforms. Uniform colors tended to be drab and practical because they were chosen to provide camouflage in the field.

Tropical uniforms for Wrens (Women's Royal Naval Service) came in cool, light-colored cotton.

A German *Stabshelferin* wore field gray, while a U.S. servicewoman might wear brown. Usually, women's uniforms featured a skirt rather than trousers. Otherwise, military women dressed very much like military men. Their shoes were flat and built for comfort. Buttoned pockets provided storage space for vital papers or equipment. Badges stitched onto a uniform's lapels, shoulders, or sleeves indicated the servicewoman's rank.

DESIGNERS DO THEIR PART

Fashion designers helped the war effort by designing uniforms. After closing his Parisian salon, Chicago-born Mainbocher (1891–1976) returned to the United States to design part of the Women's Red Cross uniform. Irish designer Digby Morton (1906–1983) designed uniforms for the Women's Voluntary Service (WVS).

Pilots no longer wore fancy braided uniforms. They wore bomber jackets.

BOMBER JACKETS

Called bomber jackets in Britain and battle jackets in the United States, these short, warm, military-issue jackets were made of thick leather or wool. They became popular with young people in the 1950s and are now worn by young and old alike.

The U.S. Marines' cap could be worn two different ways. Even in uniform, women tried to create a unique look.

ON CIVVY STREET

Not surprisingly, civilian clothes took on a military look. Uniforms were a source of inspiration for designers, and classic, tailored suits were popular. Although the lines changed only a little from the late 1930s, skirts became shorter, shoulders squarer, trousers slimmer, and shoes sturdier. For practical reasons, many more women started to wear trousers. By 1945, the silhouette had softened a little, but, in general, fashion did not change much during the war because there simply were not enough resources for people to buy new clothes each season. They bought clothes only when their old ones wore out.

Rationing and "Making Do"

To buy groceries, a customer needed a ration book. Rationing stopped people from buying more than their fair share of goods.

During World War II, enemy submarines often sank merchant ships carrying clothing or materials, and clothing manufacturers concentrated on making uniforms rather than civilian clothes.

NOT ENOUGH TO GO AROUND

There was also a shortage of labor. People who had worked as tailors and dressmakers, or in textile and clothing factories, were now in better-paid war-related work. When stocks of clothes made before the war ran out, the government had to act.

FAIR SHARE FOR ALL

In Britain, rationing was introduced on June 1, 1941, and continued until March 1949. During World War I, high prices effectively kept people from buying too much, but poorer people were unable to buy enough. For World War II, the government wanted to ensure that, regardless of income, everyone had a fair share of the limited resources.

In the 1940s, wearing seamed stockings was the fashion, but they were hard to come by. Some women made do by drawing seams on their bare legs!

COUPONS FOR CLOTHES

Everyone was given a ration book full of coupons. At first, each person got sixty-six coupons a year, but, as shortages intensified, the number was reduced. To make a sale, shops had to collect the right number of coupons as well as the correct amount of money. Whatever the price, similar items required the same number of coupons. Any man's jacket, for example, required 26 coupons; a blouse, 12 coupons; a pair of men's shoes, 18 coupons. When the coupons were gone, purchases stopped until the next ration book was issued.

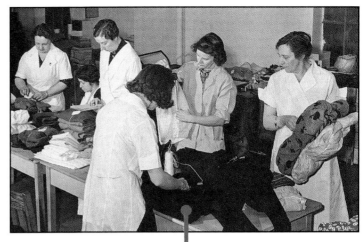

American charities collected second-hand clothes to send to people in war-torn Europe.

THRIFTY SHOPPERS

Rationing made impulse buying a thing of the past. People thought hard about what they bought, fearful they might run out of essential items, such as shoes. Most people used all their coupons, but some people sold their coupons for cash or persuaded friends in ration-free countries to send them clothes. Although rationing stopped wealthy people from getting all the clothes, it did not stop manufacturers from using scarce fabrics in clothes only the rich could afford.

For the first time, people were urged to mix and match colors to make the best use of scarce material.

MAKING NEW FROM OLD

Unless their homes — and wardrobes — were destroyed in an air raid, people had clothes from before the war. In June 1943, *Vogue* featured a dress by American designer Count René Willaumez that looked as if it were made of scarfs sewn together. Readers were encouraged to copy the effect by seaming together their own scarfs. The magazine also provided patterns for ten different items of clothing that could be made from a pre-war evening dress!

Magazines were filled with bright ideas for giving old, tired clothes a new look.

Utility Fashion

Rationing alone was not enough to ensure that clothing was fairly priced and that manufacturers were not wasteful with cloth such as silk, which was needed for parachutes. In Britain, these problems were addressed by the Utility Scheme; in the United States, the L85 laws imposed limits on the use of silk and wool.

This 1941 Vogue cover featured a trouser suit, unheard of before 1940.

STEPS TO UTILITY

Top British designers, including Hardy Amies, Norman Hartnell (who later designed the Queen's wedding dress), Edward Molyneux, Digby Morton, Victor Stiebel, and Bianca Mosca, worked on the development of Utility clothing. The plan was to design a practical, durable wardrobe consisting of a coat, suit, shirt or blouse, and dress.

RULES AND REGULATIONS

The Utility Scheme controlled the price and quality of eighty-five percent of all manufactured cloth, and clothes had to conform to strict regulations. The number of seams and pleats and the length of stitching were controlled, and a dress could not have more than two pockets or five buttons. Designs could be rejected if they were not simple enough.

Non-Utility designers also created practical clothing. In 1943, Jaeger presented this suit of green tweed and striped flannel.

The Board of Trade unveiled the sensible new Utility fashions in 1942. The first and third suits (above, from left) were the original designs; the second and fourth suits were the mass-produced versions.

INTO PRODUCTION

Once designs had been chosen, manufacturers needed licenses to mass-produce them. The government made sure license-holders received the bulk of the raw materials that could be spared for civilian use. In return, manufacturers promised to follow the Utility patterns to the letter and to obey strict guidelines on quantity and price. At first, they had misgivings about the Scheme, but they soon supported it because all the clothes they produced sold out — they never had surplus stock.

UTILITY FOR ALL

Utility clothing quickly gained a reputation for durability. The Scheme continued after the war, until about 1952, long after rationing had stopped. Not all clothes produced at the time were Utility, but even non-Utility, hand-tailored clothes were sometimes made from long-lasting Utility fabrics.

The Utility Scheme controlled furniture manufacturing, too.

UTILITY IN THE HOME

Many homes were furnished with Utility, and even Wedgwood, the pottery firm, participated — with Victory Ware! This line of crockery was designed for "simplicity of manufacture and minimum breakage."

Utility clothes were designed to survive the toughest jobs as women began to wield tools such as pitchforks and blowtorches.

Dancing the Night Away

Glenn Miller (1904–1944) was the biggest musical star of the war years.

GLENN MILLER

Known for his "sweet" sound, Glenn Miller led a string of popular orchestras. His hits included "Moonlight Serenade," "Little Brown Jug," and "In the Mood." In 1942, he formed the Glenn Miller Air Force Band to entertain the troops. He died in 1944, when his plane was shot down over the English Channel.

The war made people more determined than ever to have a good time. Death was so commonplace that people wanted to "live for today." After a long week working in a munitions factory or finally home on leave, people wanted to go out and dance their cares away. They had no evening wear, so civilians put on their best outfits, and military men and women wore uniforms.

AMERICA TAKES THE LEAD

Swing was the thing. Glenn Miller, Benny Goodman, Artie Shaw, and other star bandleaders sold millions of records. For slower dances, there were numbers by crooners such as Bing Crosby, or sentimental tearjerkers by Vera Lynn.

British women were bused to dances as partners for U.S. soldiers. Most women owned only one pair of shoes, and the shoes were practical rather than elegant.

To swing 1940s-style, couples held one or both hands as they took a step to each side. Then they did a couple of shimmies or shuffles.

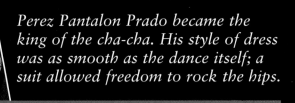

Perez Pantalon Prado became the king of the cha-cha. His style of dress was as smooth as the dance itself; a suit allowed freedom to rock the hips.

JITTERBUGGING GIs

Along with abundant supplies of nylon stockings, U.S. soldiers, nicknamed *GIs* (short for "government issue"), brought the jitterbug, or jive, to Europe. Performed to a jazz tempo, it was a fast, jerky dance that often became acrobatic!

In 1949, Parisian students jitterbugged, too, but the look was different. Baseball shoes provided great grip.

LATIN LOVERS

By the early 1950s, the cha-cha was all the rage. Invented by Cuban bandleader Enrique Jorrín, this fast dance was similar to the mambo. Looking to Latin America, an area untouched by the war, was a form of escapism, and the clothes had a holiday feel. Women wore off-the-shoulder dresses, and men wore loose-fitting suits.

By the late 1950s, everyone was jiving. In the summer of 1957, two thousand young people, in a dance marathon on board a boat, jived their way across the English Channel.

Hollywood Glamour

Wearing a thick sheepskin coat, this Vogue *cover girl of 1943 was the epitome of Hollywood chic. The number of buttons on her vest, however, was quite extravagant for the time!*

Many wartime jobs done by women meant hard work in dirty conditions. They wore unflattering jodhpurs and dungarees or men's overalls and, for safety, tied back their hair or wrapped it in a turban. After the initial excitement of wearing workmen's clothes, however, many women longed for a Ginger Rogers' gown or Veronica Lake's flowing, wavy hair. Such luxuries were impractical, and some were impossible to come by, but they could be admired from afar on the silver screen.

MORALE-BOOSTING MOVIES

Although the cinema offered news and information, most moviegoers sought entertainment and escapism. Women, in particular, wanted to soak up the extravagant elegance of movie stars.

Governments understood that the cinema was an important way for people to take their minds off the war. So film companies were allowed to buy some of the limited luxury cloth and use it to make fashions for film stars that disregarded the strict regulations on style.

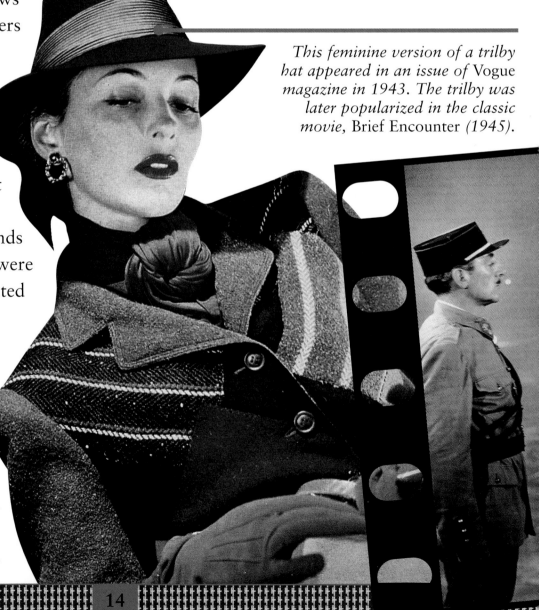

This feminine version of a trilby hat appeared in an issue of Vogue *magazine in 1943. The trilby was later popularized in the classic movie,* Brief Encounter *(1945).*

SCREEN ROMANCE

Romantic films were the best form of escapism. Classics, such as *Casablanca* (1942), were shot in moody black and white.

In 1942, magazine readers were urged to inexpensively recreate the film-star feel of these New York suits by wearing real flowers as accessories.

REALITY ON THE BIG SCREEN

America entered the war after the Japanese bombed the U.S. naval base at Pearl Harbor, Hawaii, in 1941. News of such events was spread through the cinema. Between the featured films, short newsreels were shown — to inspire patriotism.

A small boat is moving in to rescue crew members from the USS West Virginia.

Bette Davis and Joan Crawford were smolderingly sophisticated, and musicals, such as *Cover Girl*, starring Rita Hayworth, featured frivolous fashions.

HOMESPUN GLAMOUR

Magazines tried to convey the drama of Hollywood on their pages. They suggested ways to dress up plain clothes and featured eye-catching advertisements and tips on how to apply makeup. Makeup, which was availablc in shops, was one way for a woman to grab a little slice of glamour. Women copied their film-star heroines' makeup techniques.

Despite Casablanca's *war-time setting, its stars, Ingrid Bergman and Humphrey Bogart, oozed glamour.*

Paris Fights Back

After Paris was liberated, French designers put on a traveling Théâtre de la Mode *(fashion show) to promote Parisian couture.*

Pre-war Paris had been considered the capital of the fashion world. In the summer of 1940, however, the city was occupied by German soldiers, and Paris was suddenly cut off from the rest of the world.

BEHIND THE LINES

Designers who were not French, such as Charles Creed, Mainbocher, Edward Molyneux, and Elsa Schiaparelli, left France. French-born Coco Chanel closed her boutique, but stayed in Paris. Jacques Heim, who was Jewish, went into hiding. Over ninety couturiers, however, stayed open. Designers Pierre Balmain, Christian Dior, Lucien Lelong, and Nina Ricci all continued to work in Nazi-occupied Paris, selling to the wives and mistresses of Nazi officers.

Streets and cafés in Paris were crowded with German soldiers on Bastille Day in July 1940. Paris was occupied for four years.

This Schiaparelli outfit was featured in her 1945 collection. The scarf was a patriotic design in red, white, and blue.

LIBERTÉ!

After Paris was liberated, in August 1944, American *Vogue* did a feature on Paris fashions. While British and American designers had simplified their clothes, Paris couturiers had continued in their pre-war, opulent style. *Vogue*'s editor, Edna Woolman Chase, said French designers had been patriotic by wasting Nazi labor and materials. Even so, many wealthy European women shunned Parisian couture.

The French look included costly furs and the lavish use of silks for gloves and hats.

A TRAVELING FASHION SHOW

To renew interest in Parisian fashion, Paris designers created the *Théâtre de la Mode*, a traveling exhibition of tiny mannequins, displaying designers' garments in miniature. The show started in Paris and then toured America and Europe. It was a huge success and drew attention back to Parisian couture. Only Dior's "New Look," however, would win back international clients.

For the collections of 1945, many designers returned to Paris. This outfit from Schiaparelli's show had a high beaver-felt hat and a chin-hugging scarf. These items were described as "Directoire" because they recalled the styles that were popular when France was at the height of its power, in the Directorate period (1795–1799).

THE DE-MOB SUIT

At the end of the war, people leaving the armed forces had few civilian clothes. In Britain, a demobilization clothing program was set up. Ex-servicewomen received a cash allowance and clothing coupons, but men were given a "de-mob" outfit consisting of a suit, an overcoat, a shirt with two detachable collars, a tie, two pairs of socks, a pair of shoes, and a hat. Some men wore de-mob clothes well into the 1950s because they were unable to buy replacements.

De-mob clothes were mass-produced to Utility specifications — sturdy but not stylish.

Dior and the New Look

This 1947 Dior design has the classic New Look silhouette. A wool coat reveals flowing taffeta pleats.

By 1947, despite the initial outrage at the extravagance of wartime French couture, women everywhere were tired of practical fashions. Sensing the mood, Christian Dior set up his own fashion house, backed by textile industrialist Marcel Boussac.

Few women could afford a mink collar, but Dior's feminine New Look shape was loved and copied by many.

FEMININITY IN FASHION

On February 12, 1947, Dior unveiled his "New Look." Its essence was sloping shoulders, a tight bodice, a tiny waist, and a full, billowing skirt that reached to mid-calf. This look created a feminine, hourglass figure that was set off with simple jewelry, silk stockings, and stiletto-heeled shoes. Other essential accessories included a hat, often worn to one side, and long gloves. Dior's New Look marked a return to elegance — and women adored it.

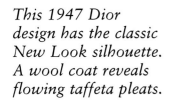

From its huge hat and big collar to its tiny, pinched waist, this outfit from Piguet (1947) had a top-heavy look.

To achieve the perfect figure, women wore lace-up corsets or bras and girdles. Some underwear had bone strips for support; some used strong elastics.

LAVISH OR WASTEFUL?

Dior had set out to "liberate all women from a poverty-stricken era." Including petticoats, each New Look outfit required up to 49 yards (45 meters) of fabric. By comparison, less than 3 yards (3 m) were needed for a typical British wartime dress. Although the war was over, British women could only marvel at the New Look because rationing was still part of their lives. The Junior Trade Minister said the new fashion was "irresponsibly frivolous and wasteful," but, when manufacturing regulations were lifted, the New Look was adapted for mass-production — a straight-skirted version was introduced.

FOUNDATIONS FOR FASHION

To achieve the New Look silhouette, women had to be as extravagant with their underwear as with their outerwear. Dior stated firmly, "Without foundations, there can be no fashion." Ample petticoats created the full skirt, but it had to be accentuated with a tiny waist.

CORSET CONTROL

Corsets came back into fashion. In 1946, Marcel Rochas introduced a new version called the waspie, or waist cincher. It covered only the waist, but the whalebone used for shaping was extremely uncomfortable. Before long, roll-on girdles were used. They had clever stitching to hold the figure firmly in place.

This Molyneux dress (1947) had tiered three-quarter-length sleeves and rounded shoulders, with a soft sash draping from the hip.

THE BIKINI AND THE BOMB

Not all Paris fashions used an excess of material. In 1946, designer Louis Réard and couturier Jacques Heim both created skimpy two-piece swimsuits. Heim christened his the *atome*. On July 1, 1946, the United States conducted its first atomic test on Bikini Atoll in the Pacific. It tore the island in two, and the *atome* soon became known as the "bikini."

A contestant for France's "Most Beautiful Bather of 1946" modeled the new bikini.

Sloping shoulders were not new. Molyneux had used them in 1941 with the loose raglan sleeves of this flowing yellow coat.

Rebels *without* a Cause

After the hard years of the 1940s, the 1950s heralded wealth, disposable income, and confidence. Servicemen who had returned from the war and started families caused a baby boom that swelled the teenage population from the mid-1950s. With most young people living at home, and plenty of work to go around, there suddenly was more spending power than ever before.

FASHION STATEMENT

As young people became better educated, they developed a political and social conscience. Working-class youths in Britain expressed their views on social injustice by adopting the Saville Row dress of the upper-class "nobs." These teddy boys, as they were called, strutted around in thick-soled shoes and tailored suits.

The drape jackets and drainpipe trousers of the teddy boys were supposed to be a revival of men's fashions during the reign of King Edward VII. A first step toward a classless society, the "yobs" were imitating the "nobs."

RESTLESS YOUTH

Between 1956 and 1961, eight movies had titles that included the word *teenager*. Still more had restless youth as their subjects. *Lost, Lonely, and Vicious* (1958) showed American teenagers racing around in cars and hanging out in groups.

HOT RODDERS

Whether a motorcycle, a motorbike, or a car, a rebel had to have an independent — and fast — means of transportation. In the United States, a new craze called hot rodding developed. Cars were customized for optimum speed. All the non-essentials were stripped off to leave a mean speed machine. Hot rod clubs sprang up across the U.S.

A Seattle hot rodder installed four new carburetors so his engine would make a head-turning noise.

Marlon Brando appeared as a drag-racing teenage rebel in The Wild One *(1954).*

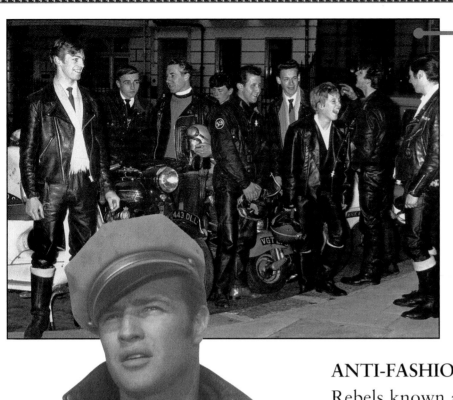

The uniform of Britain's ton-up boys included a black leather jacket and big biker boots. Leather was scarce, however, so some made do with cheap black vinyl.

James Dean played the typical teenage rebel in Rebel Without a Cause. *His mission was to "live fast and die young." Tragically, Dean was killed in a car accident on September 30, 1955.*

ANTI-FASHION

Rebels known as bikers in the United States and ton-up boys in Britain dismissed suits altogether. They wore tough work clothes that could withstand the time they spent on a motorcycle. The items that became the most popular and enduring were leather jackets, jeans, and T-shirts, like those worn by screen rebels and idols, such as Marlon Brando and James Dean.

THE FIRST LEVI'S

Levi Strauss first introduced jeans to the United States in the 1850s. He sold his dyed-denim trousers to the gold rushers as work wear. Today, jeans are worn by just about everyone — not just teenage rebels.

T-shirts were first worn by U.S. soldiers, then by workmen. They were adopted by rebellious youths during the 1950s.

America and Consumerism

With Paris closed during the war, American designers could no longer seek inspiration from the semi-annual French shows. So they started to make their own casual clothes and sports-wear. Their styles were ideal for the increasingly active roles of women and were easily mass-produced.

Post-war America idealized the model nuclear family, in which women were homemakers who kept their homes, their children, and themselves neat and tidy.

THE ALL-AMERICAN FAMILY

After the war, new technologies, such as television sets, refrigerators, automatic washers, and cars, became available to almost every middle-class family in America. These new consumer goods took care of day-to-day drudgery, freeing women to spend more time on looking good. In her films, Doris Day portrayed the new female role — the model wife in coordinating pastel separates.

The comfortable twinset always looked good. Pastel shades were considered the most feminine. A boxy handbag completed the look.

PRACTICAL DAY WEAR

Since the 1850s, when Amelia Bloomer (1818–1894) pioneered Turkish-style ladies' trousers, the United States has been at the forefront of producing practical clothing for women.

The most-influential American fashion designer of the 1950s was Claire McCardell (1905–1958). Her clothes were sporty, relaxed, comfortable, and functional. She worked with simple fabrics, such as cotton, jersey, denim, and chambray. Neat gingham checks were a popular pattern. Other hallmarks were the wraparound dress and the softly pleated, full dirndl skirt. The emphasis was on health, fitness, and sport.

Paris took note. With his 1958 bonbonnière collection, shoemaker Charles Jourdan celebrated the candy box colors so popular in the United States — pineapple yellow, cherry pink, and glacier blue.

McCardell's swimwear used soft fabrics and had a natural shape.

COMFORT AT LAST

Beginning in the late 1920s, Claire McCardell developed what became known as the American Look. McCardell designed practical, comfortable clothes for active women, taking simple shapes and superimposing them with pockets, contrasting topstitching, hooks, and rivets.

MIX AND MATCH SEPARATES

Another American designer who pioneered functional clothing was Bonnie Cashin (*b.* 1915). She worked with leather, canvas, poplin, suede, and tweed and created easy-to-wear kimonos, tabards, ponchos, hooded coats, and long, mohair-fringed skirts. Her layered clothes were the direct opposite of Dior's carefully assembled New Look. Instead, a woman's wardrobe consisted of brightly colored separates that could be mixed and matched to create a variety of comfortable outfits suitable for any occasion.

COMPLETING THE LOOK

Dressing casually meant that, before long, hats were out of style. Cosmetics, on the other hand, became more popular than ever. Everyone had to have penciled eyebrows, mascara-laden lashes, and luscious, glossy lips.

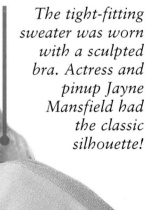

The tight-fitting sweater was worn with a sculpted bra. Actress and pinup Jayne Mansfield had the classic silhouette!

Zooties, Hipsters, and Beatniks

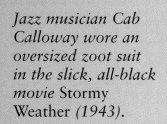

Jazz musician Cab Calloway wore an oversized zoot suit in the slick, all-black movie Stormy Weather *(1943).*

Two basic trends developed in underground fashion of the period — dressing up and dressing down. As a rule, underground chic aimed to help people escape the class they started out in.

BIRTH OF THE ZOOT SUIT

Long before modernists emerged in the late 1940s, a flamboyant suit-wearing style flourished on the streets of Harlem, New York. Underprivileged blacks and Mexicans who had "made good" dressed up in baggy suits, called zoot suits, that came in a rainbow of peacock colors. The zoot suit became the uniform of all top jazz stars of the day, but zooties were criticized during the war, when clothing restrictions were established. Public outcry over the waste of valuable material led to zoot suit riots. They began in Los Angeles in 1943, when white servicemen attacked and tore the suits off some Mexican-American zooties. The riots spread quickly to other major U.S. cities. With their own zootie style, known as *zazou*, the French ignored clothing restrictions imposed by German occupiers, and they suffered attacks similar to those in the United States.

In the 1950s, Thelonius Monk's baggy-suited jazz band was photographed outside Minton's Playhouse in Harlem, the birthplace of bebop.

GROOVY HIPSTERS

After the war, a new form of jazz, called bebop, became popular. More experimental than the swing of the zooties, bebop stars included Thelonius Monk and Charlie Parker. Suits were slimmer than the zoot but were still baggy and in wild fabrics. Dizzy Gillespie's leopardskin jacket was legendary. Berets were popular, and "shades" were a must. Hipsters had their own sound, look, and slang; clothes, for example, were called "threads."

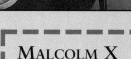
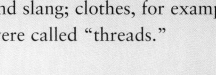

Members of Machito's rhythm section are wearing "Cool School" collarless jackets. By the late 1940s, jazz had become associated with the sleek modernist look.

THE BEAT GENERATION

Hipsters were not the only ones to "dig" jazz. Beatniks loved jazz and its counterpart, poetry. Leaders of this tradition, started in Paris by philosopher Jean-Paul Sartre, were author Jack Kerouac and poet Alan Ginsberg. Ginsberg later coined the popular term "flower power." The bohemian fashion of the time involved dressing down, and black was a favorite color. Women wore men's shirts over tight pedal pushers or trousers. Hair was cut short. By the end of the 1950s, the bohemian look had reached Hollywood, most notably in *Breakfast at Tiffany's* (1961), starring Audrey Hepburn.

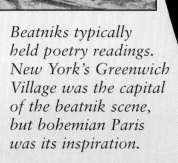

Beatniks typically held poetry readings. New York's Greenwich Village was the capital of the beatnik scene, but bohemian Paris was its inspiration.

French model Capucine wore beatnik pedal pushers with an oversized shirt (1958). "Must-have" footwear had wedged heels and ballet straps.

MALCOLM X

Fashions can make powerful political statements. The zoot suits of the early 1940s were one of the earliest expressions of black pride. It is not surprising, then, that Malcolm X (1925–1965) was, in his time, a zootie.

Civil rights activist Malcolm X was shot to death at a rally in 1965.

Rock 'n' Roll and the New Youth Culture

The summer of 1955 witnessed the birth of a momentous new musical style — rock 'n' roll. Originating in the United States, it fused the sounds of country and western with rhythm and blues. To go with this wild new music were wild new looks for its young fans.

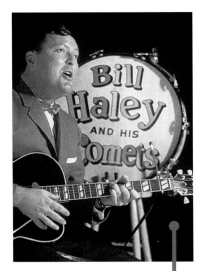

Bill Haley and the Comets' Rock Around the Clock (1955) marked the birth of rock 'n' roll.

SODA-FOUNTAIN STYLE

Teenage fans of rock 'n' roll wore clothes to show off on the dance floor. Full, knee-length skirts with tight, elastic, cinch belts were worn over layers of nylon-net petticoats. More often than not, the skirts sported checks or large polka dots. Bobby socks and flat shoes completed the outfit. Girls often wore their hair tied up in a ponytail, which would flick from side to side as they danced the energetic new steps.

Elvis was famous for his two-tone shoes as well as for the way he moved his hips when he sang.

JUKEBOX JURY

The meeting place for teenagers in the United States was the soda fountain, where a jukebox played all the latest tunes. In Britain, teenagers met at the coffee bar.

Teenagers played their favorite records on a jukebox.

ROCKABILLY KING

Elvis Presley performed to hordes of screaming teenage fans. His southern rock 'n' roll style later came to be known as rockabilly. Rockabilly was unusual in that it embraced two opposite styles of dress — hipster and biker. Elvis would appear in a suit and two-tone shoes one day, then in torn jeans and a T-shirt the next. Rockabilly boys usually wore suits in pastel shades that had a patterned shirt with an oversized collar underneath. Rockabilly girls were as much at home in their denims as in a neat suit, and they wore stylish accessories, such as patterned silk scarfs and designer sunglasses.

Rockabilly boys wore their hair slicked back. Girls tied theirs back with ribbons. Clean-cut rockabillies made a comeback in the late 1970s.

INTO THE SWINGING '60s

As the 1950s came to a close, it was clear that fashion, particularly youth styles, would continue to spin off in every direction. Teenagers were individuals in their own right, not content with copying the styles of their parents. Their individualism would lead to some outrageous outfits, often worn to shock the older generation, and with pop music so central to the new youth culture, the concert stage would, in the future, be as important to fashion as the catwalk.

Flared skirts worn with tight-fitting sweaters showed off the figure but also allowed freedom of movement.

At the soda fountain, teenagers bought soft drinks and danced to the latest rock 'n' roll.

The Technology of Fashion

In 1939, most garments were still made individually in small workshops. A single worker assembled an entire garment, much as a couturier does today. Although it produced unique clothing, this method was not very efficient.

To make nylons keep their shape, they were eased onto metal molds, then subjected to very hot steam.

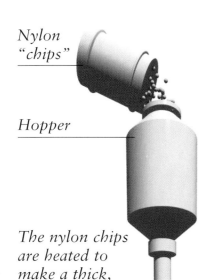

Nylon "chips"

Hopper

The nylon chips are heated to make a thick, sticky fluid.

Cold air hardens the nylon thread.

The nylon is forced through a spinneret.

Hot steam sets, or fixes, the thread.

Nylon filaments are twisted into yarn and rolled onto a bobbin.

FASHION IN BULK

Mass-production methods developed before World War II were now being used by many big clothing firms. Wartime governments had wanted a high percentage of clothing to be made this way to ensure that scarce materials and workers were used as efficiently as possible. The British Board of Trade, for example, issued the majority of its Utility licenses to firms that would mass-produce.

THE FIRST SYNTHETIC

The fabric of the age was nylon, the very first synthetic. Patented in 1937, nylon went into production at Du Pont's New Jersey plant in 1938. It was first used to make toothbrush bristles.

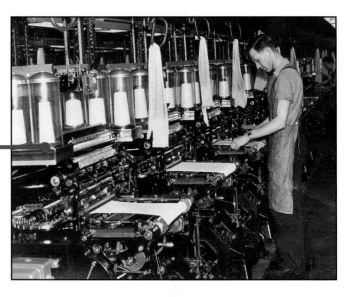

By 1949, new high-tech knitting machines, such as these at a factory in Enniskillen, Northern Ireland, could produce ten thousand nylon stockings a day.

in the 1940s and 1950s

Nylon could be spun to a much finer gauge than silk. The machine for spinning even the finest silk needed at least 540 needles. The machine for spinning nylon needed only 400.

In 1939, Du Pont started spinning nylon yarn for stockings. The first nylon stockings, or "nylons," went on sale in the United States in May 1940. All four million pairs sold out in four days. Nylon transformed the textile industry. It was easy to dye, and its color did not fade. Unlike silk, it did not wrinkle or bag, and it did not attract moths.

SUPER FABRIC!

From 1941, when the United States entered the war, until 1945, very few nylon stockings were manufactured. The first British-made nylons went on sale in 1946, and, soon after that, versatile nylon was being mixed with other natural fibers to make many kinds of clothing, including dresses, blouses, suits, ties, and undergarments. Du Pont continued to experiment with this new textile and, in the late 1950s, created a fireproof nylon, called aramid, that would be used to clothe firefighters and race car drivers.

The Caprice bra (1955) was made of nylon taffeta and nylon lace. The elastic net girdle controlled the body for a sleek silhouette, and its garters held up nylon stockings.

Fashions for a feminine figure made liberal use of synthetic nylon and manufactured rayon fabrics.

· T I M E L I N E ·

	FASHION	WORLD EVENTS	TECHNOLOGY	FAMOUS PEOPLE	ART & MEDIA
1940	•U.S.: first nylon stockings on sale	•World War II continues (1939–1945)		•McDonald brothers set up first hamburger stand	•Stravinsky: Symphony in C major
1941		•Japanese attack Pearl Harbor; U.S. enters war	•First aerosol spray cans •Terylene thread invented	•James Joyce dies	•Brecht: Mother Courage •Coward: Blithe Spirit
1942	•Utility Scheme begins •U.S. Navy issue T-shirt	•Oxfam founded	•First nuclear reactor built in U.S.	•Gandhi imprisoned by British in India	•Bergman and Bogart star in Casablanca
1943	•Zoot suit riots begin •Cashin in Hollywood	•Mussolini arrested			•Sartre: Being and Nothingness
1944	•McCardell designs pumps	•Allies land in France and drive back Germans		•Glenn Miller dies in plane crash	•Henry Moore: Mother and Child
1945	•Théâtre de la Mode tours U.S. and Europe	•Germany and Japan surrender; war ends	•First atomic bombs •Microwave oven patented	•U.S.: Truman elected president •Suicide of Hitler	•Britten: Peter Grimes •Steinbeck: Cannery Row
1946	•Rochas: waspie •First bikinis	•UN General Assembly holds first meetings	•ENIAC: first universal electronic computer		•Picasso: Reclining Nude •O'Neill: The Iceman Cometh
1947	•Dior unveils New Look	•India and Pakistan gain independence	•Yeager breaks sound barrier in U.S. Bell X-1	•Nehru becomes India's first prime minister	•Cannes Film Festival opens •Camus: The Plague
1948		•S. Africa: apartheid begins •Israel proclaimed	•Transistor invented •Frisbee patented	•Gandhi assassinated	•Huston: Key Largo •John Wayne in Red River
1949	•Schiaparelli opens house in New York	•NATO formed •East and West Germany formed		•Mao proclaims Chinese People's Republic	•Eames house completed •Orwell: 1984
1950		•Korean War begins •China invades Tibet	•First credit card company, Diners Club, founded	•U.S.: McCarthyism begins	•Jackson Pollock: Autumn Rhythm
1951	•Balmain opens ready-to-wear branches in U.S.		•First video recording demonstrated		•Festival of Britain •The African Queen
1952	•Utility Scheme ends	•Kenya: Mau Mau revolt begins		•Elizabeth II proclaimed Queen on father's death	•Le Corbusier: Unité d'Habitation
1953	•Hartnell: Elizabeth II's coronation gown	•Korean War ends •Egypt: Nasser in power	•Crick and Watson describe DNA structure	•Hillary and Norgay climb Mt. Everest	•Osborne: Look Back in Anger •Miller: The Crucible
1954	•Chanel reopens her Paris Fashion house	•SEATO formed	•Trials of contraceptive pill start	•Roger Bannister runs four-minute mile	•Kingsley Amis: Lucky Jim •Brando in The Wild One
1955	•Mary Quant opens Bazaar	•Warsaw Pact formed •South Africa leaves UN	•Hovercraft patented •Optical fibers patented	•Einstein dies •James Dean dies in car accident	•Patrick White: Tree of Man •Hitchcock: Rear Window
1956	•Balenciaga designs "sack" dress	•Suez crisis in Middle East		•Elvis Presley's Heartbreak Hotel tops U.S. record charts	•Beckett: Waiting for Godot
1957	•Vogue editor Edna Chase Woolman dies	•EEC (Common Market) founded	•USSR launches first satellite, Sputnik 1	•Macmillan succeeds Eden as British prime minister	•Chagall: The Circus Rider •Kerouac: On the Road
1958	•School of Fashion, RCA •Claire McCardell dies	•Anti-bomb protests start	•Heart pacemaker invented •First hula hoop	•De Gaulle elected president of France	•Chevalier and Caron star in Gigi
1959	•Du Pont trademarks Lycra	•Cuba: Castro in power •U.S. troops sent to Laos	•Silicon chips first made •Austin mini launched	•Buddy Holly dies in plane crash	•Mies van der Rohe: Seagram Building

Glossary

chambray: a lightweight fabric with colored and white threads interwoven for a mottled effect.

dirndl: a full, gathered skirt with a tight waistband.

drainpipe trousers: men's trousers with narrow, tight legs, also called "stovepipe" trousers or pants.

drape jacket: a long, waistless, woolen jacket with velvet-trimmed collar, cuffs, and pockets, typically worn by Britain's teddy boys.

girdle: a tight, elasticized woman's undergarment that extends from the waist to the thighs.

mass-production: producing goods in very large quantities, usually by using machinery.

modernist style: the sleek look of the 1950s, when men wore slim, single-breasted, sometimes collarless suits and button-down shirts with narrow ties.

pedal pushers: calf-length trousers for women and girls.

raglan: a style of sleeve that is sewn in along two diagonal seams running from the neck to the armpit.

roll-on: a tight, elastic, girdle-style corset with special stitching to effectively compress the stomach.

Saville Row: a street in London famous for its tailors.

spinneret: a small tube through which a thick "nylon" fluid is forced to produce nylon thread.

stiletto heel: a high and very thin heel on women's shoes.

swing: a smooth, lively, orchestral type of jazz that has been popular since the 1930s.

tabard: a hip-length, sleeveless, rectangular woman's top, with a hole for the head to go through.

taffeta: a stiff, shiny fabric of various woven fibers.

waspie: a short, rigid, boned corset, extending from the bottom of the ribs to the top of the hips and, sometimes, lacing up the back.

More Books to Read

The 1940s. The 1950s. Fashion Sourcebooks (series). John Peacock (Thames and Hudson)

The Art of Haute Couture. Victor Skrebneski and Laura Jacobs (Abbeville Press)

Christian Dior: The Man Who Made the World Look New. Marie France Pochna (Arcade)

Costume Since 1945: Couture, Street Style and Anti-Fashion. Deirdre Clancy (Drama Publishers)

Everyday Fashions of the Forties As Pictured in Sears Catalogs. JoAnne Olian, editor (Dover)

Fashions of a Decade (series). *The 1940s. The 1950s.* Patricia Baker (Facts on File)

Great Fashion Designs of the Fifties: Paper Dolls in Full Color. Tom Tierney (Dover)

Great Fashion Designs of the Forties: Paper Dolls in Full Color. Tom Tierney (Dover)

A Matter of Style: Women in the Fashion Industry. Women Then — Women Now (series). Linda Leuzzi (Franklin Watts)

Web Sites

Fitted Fifties Finery. *www.staylace.com/fff.htm*

Rationed Fashion: American fashion during World War II. *www.geocities.com/SoHo/Coffeehouse/6727/rationed_fashion.html*

Timeline of Costume History.
  20th Century Western Costume: 1940-1950
  www.costumes.org/pages/timelinepages/1940s1.htm
  20th Century Western Costume: 1950-1960
  www.costumes.org/pages/timelinepages/1950s1.htm

Due to the dynamic nature of the Internet, some web sites stay current longer than others. To find additional web sites, use a reliable search engine with one or more of the following keywords: *beatniks, clothing, costume, couturier, Dior, fabric, fashion, fashion design, girdle, hats, jazz, Levi's, McCardell, New Look, Quant, rock 'n' roll, shoes,* and *swing.*

Index